You make my world brighter
and my life sweeter.
Most of all, Grandson,
you make my heart smile.

— Linda E. Knight

Nothing Fills the Heart with Joy like a

Grandson

Words to Let a Grandson Know How Much He Is Loved

Edited by
Patricia Wayant

Blue Mountain Press™
Boulder, Colorado

We wish to thank Susan Polis Schutz for permission to reprint the following poems that appear in this publication: "Take Time To…," "I'm So Proud of You," "As you keep growing…," "Believe in Yourself and Your Dreams," "I Feel So Fortunate to Have You for a Grandson," and "A grandson is…," Copyright © 1986, 1988, 2004 by Stephen Schutz and Susan Polis Schutz. All rights reserved.

Library of Congress Control Number: 2013953061
ISBN: 978-1-59842-794-3

◪ and Blue Mountain Press are registered in U.S. Patent and Trademark Office.
Certain trademarks are used under license.

Acknowledgments appear on page 92.

Printed in China.
First Printing: 2014

♻ This book is printed on recycled paper.

This book is printed on paper that has been specially produced to be acid free (neutral pH) and contains no groundwood or unbleached pulp. It conforms with the requirements of the American National Standards Institute, Inc., so as to ensure that this book will last and be enjoyed by future generations.

Blue Mountain Arts, Inc.
P.O. Box 4549, Boulder, Colorado 80306

Contents

(Authors listed in order of first appearance)

To the Best Grandson There Could Ever Be

I could have every wonderful word in
the dictionary right by my side, but
I still wouldn't be able to completely
describe what a treasure you are to me.

You're one of the most invaluable
blessings in the whole wide world,
and you always will be.

And I just thought it might be nice
to let you know that I feel very,
very lucky to be the grandparent
of someone who is living proof that
some dreams really do come true.

I couldn't have asked for a more
wonderful grandson… than you.

— Chris Gallatin

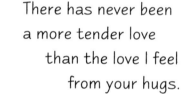

There has never been
a more beautiful sight
  than your smile
or a more endearing joy
  than your kind spirit.

There has never been
a more tender love
  than the love I feel
    from your hugs.

Your sense of humor,
depth of feeling,
and gentle nature
have drawn me closer to you
than I ever expected.

When we are together,
I am reminded of how
thankful I am
to spend time with you
and how proud I am of you.

Today and always,
I give my love to you,
along with the hope
that I can always be
a source of strength to you —
and everything else
a grandparent can be.

— Susan Hickman Sater

I'm So Proud of You

I am so happy with the direction
that your life is taking you
You are unique and special
and I know that
your talents will give you
many paths to choose from
in the future
Always keep your many interests —
they will allow your mind
to remain energized
Always keep your positive outlook —
it will give you the strength to
accomplish great things
Always keep your determination —
it will give you the ability
to succeed in meeting your goals
Always keep your excitement
about whatever you do —
it will help you to have fun

Always keep your sense of humor —
it will allow you to
make mistakes and learn from them
Always keep your confidence —
it will allow you to take risks
and not be afraid of failure
Always keep your sensitivity —
it will help you to understand
and do something about
injustices in the world
As you continue to grow
in your own unique, wonderful way
always remember that
I am more proud of you
than ever before

— Susan Polis Schutz

I've Loved You Since the Minute You Were Born

Ever since you came into this world,
I have known what perfect love is.
I am so grateful to have
a tenderhearted grandchild like you.
Whenever I look into your gleaming eyes,
I see a soul full of love and sweetness.

You and I share so much,
and I am happiest
when I'm listening to you
dream and reminisce.

Because you are a spirited person,
I know there will always be
something to smile about
whenever you are around.

I hope you know what a precious
gift of love you are to me.
Your inspiring soul
makes our family so happy,
and my heart shines with so much pride.
How lucky I am to have you
as my grandchild!
— Dianne Cogar

You Are Life's Gift of Joy to Me

You bring joy to my life and my heart.
You're an amazing person,
a wonderful grandson,
and the nicest gift I could have ever asked for.
You leave your own special "heartprint"
wherever you go.
You make a happy difference in so many ways;
the universe is blessed to have you in it.
No one else has your own brand of caring,
style of sharing, and way of being
the wonderful grandson that you are.

No one else has a smile that can
light up a thousand tomorrows.
Your warmth can never be matched.
You truly are a gift of joy to me.
I hope you will always
embrace the beauty of life,
hold your family close
and your dreams near,
and celebrate your blessings.
You make my world brighter
and my life sweeter.
Most of all, Grandson,
you make my heart smile.

— Linda E. Knight

"There is nothing more important than family."

Those seven words should be etched in stone on the sidewalks that lead to every happy home.

I feel so blessed to have a family that is filled with some of the best people this world will ever know… and one that inspires gratitude, joy, and deep appreciation.

Our family is such an essential part of my life, my dreams, my highest hopes, and my sweetest memories… and I thank you with all my heart for being such a beautiful, precious, and important part of every day!

— Douglas Pagels

Because we're family…

We have a place to go where arms are always open and hearts want to know what they can do to keep us happy, healthy, and safe.

We have a haven where we can laugh and play and renew the energies exhausted by stress and strain — a sanctuary where we can heal from pain and sorrow and find hope and faith. We have customs and traditions to keep with the people who are linked to us in history and in the precious memories we've built together.

We have a snug spot where we are always comfortable — and loved ones are gathered around to love, support, and rejoice in the highlights of our lives.

We have all the best things money could never buy… because we are family.

— Jacqueline Schiff

The Magic of Grandchildren

Grandchildren... rekindle for us the spirit of play, the child's sense of adventure and discovery. Grandparents are always being told that they are living history to their grandchildren, that they give the children the reassurance of their roots, the strengthening awareness of continuity. For me and many grandmothers I have talked to, it works the other way as well. They give <u>us</u> continuity. They link us to our own motherhood and childhood years, to our parents and grandparents and the stories we remember of times even earlier than those. And they link us to the future as well. They give us a vested interest in the world in which they will live. They make us aware of the world in which we are living today and helping to create for tomorrow.

— Ruth Goode

A grandson is...

a kite flying through the trees
a tadpole turning into a frog
a dandelion in the wind
a mischievous smile
laughing eyes
a scrape on the knees
a wonder
an excitement, a burst of energy
an animation
a spirited breeze
A grandson is love
and everything beautiful

— Susan Polis Schutz

What Is a Boy?

Between the innocence of babyhood and the dignity of manhood, we find a delightful creature called a boy. Boys come in assorted sizes, weights, and colors, but all boys have the same creed: to enjoy every second of every minute of every hour of every day and to protest with noise (their only weapon) when their last minute is finished and adult males pack them off to bed at night.

Boys are found everywhere — on top of, underneath, inside of, climbing on, swinging from, running around, or jumping to. Mothers love them, little girls hate them, older sisters and brothers tolerate them, adults ignore them, and Heaven protects them.

A boy is Truth with dirt on its face,
Beauty with a cut on its finger, Wisdom
with bubble gum in its hair, and the Hope
of the future with a frog in its pocket....

A boy is a magical creature — you can
lock him out of your workshop, but you
can't lock him out of your heart. You can
get him out of your study, but you can't
get him out of your mind. Might as well give
up — he is your captor, your jailor, your
boss, and your master — a freckled-faced,
pint-sized, cat-chasing bundle of noise.

— Alan Beck

Be Yourself, Grandson, and There's Nothing You Can't Do

Be yourself, believe in yourself, try to love everything about yourself… and you'll be respected. ♥ Take care of your body and continue to challenge your mind… and you'll be admired. ♥ Don't listen to anyone who questions your dreams or your choices. ♥ Be your own leader… and others will follow you. ♥ Make the most of every moment, embrace every opportunity, and take lots of pictures… There's so much you'll want to remember. ♥ Take chances, trust your instincts, and never give up on your dreams. ♥

— Charley Knox

As you keep growing and learning
striving and searching
it is very important
that you pursue your own interests
without anything holding you back
It will take time
to fully understand yourself
and to discover what you
want out of life
As you keep growing and learning
striving and searching
I know that the steps in your journey
will take you on the right path

— Susan Polis Schutz

My Grandson Learns
How to Punctuate

At the end of his school day,
he climbs into my car,
this kindergarten child whose
birth almost eluded us
as we watched his mother
contract too soon.

He snaps his seatbelt, this
dimpled imp whose sweet
voice belies the grit that
helped him hang on until
his scheduled delivery date.

He talks of his day —
the art of learning, his
discovery of words on the page,
the read-aloud poem of the week
requiring three adult signatures.

He tells of his highlight,
*Nana, he says, today I learned
all about punctuation, I know*
    the period
    the question mark
    the excabation point.

But, he confides, *I didn't
learn about the comma yet.*
Reaching his home, he hops
from the car, mounts the stairs
toward his snack in the kitchen,

this after-school gift,
my brown-eyed
excabation point.

                 — Gail Fishman Gerwin

Grandson, You Are Meant for Greatness

In you, I see courage and strength
and the willingness
to meet life's challenges.
I honor your risk taking,
creativity, and zest for living.
I enjoy your free spirit
and your offbeat sense of humor.
I'm inspired by your example.
I know great things are in store for you.
I celebrate who you are,
what you have done,
and all the amazing potential
that is yet to be realized.
You deserve the very best life has to offer.

— Candy Paull

A man is as great as the dreams he dreams,
as great as the love he bears;
As great as the values he redeems
and the happiness he shares.
A man is as great as the thoughts he thinks,
as the worth he has attained;
As the fountains at which his spirit drinks
and the insight he has gained.
A man is as great as the truth he speaks,
as great as the help he gives,
As great as the destiny he seeks,
as great as the life he lives.

— C. E. Flynn

Trust in Yourself

There are paths to greatness that are easy to find, but once you get on them and start traveling, you must look deep inside your heart to figure out the best way to go.

When searching for the great role that you will play in this world, you've got to give it your all and then some more! There are easier roads to travel, but only the roads that lead to greatness of heart and mind will give you the satisfaction and happiness that you are seeking within your soul.

Breathe deep, look inside yourself, and you
will discover the right steps to lead you where
you really want to go. You've got everything
it takes to be all that you can be. Trust
in yourself and you can never go wrong.

— Ashley Rice

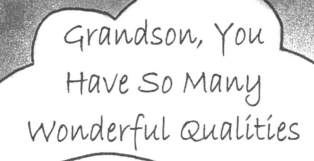

Grandson, You Have So Many Wonderful Qualities

You are strong. Whenever adversity finds you, you face it with confidence and assurance.

You are kind. You speak up for those who are down, be they friends or strangers. You are fair and open-minded.

You are generous. You reach out to people with your heart and take them in. You give friendship and love freely, with the attitude of someone who knows that the supply of those things never runs out.

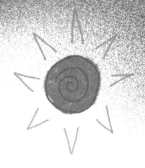

You are full of happiness. You find joy in so many things, large and small, and you teach those around you to find it too. Because of you, I see a brighter and better world.

You are a source of light. When life is going badly and things look grim, you are always there to turn my eyes toward the positive, encourage me, and help me find my path forward.

You are so wonderful in so many ways.

— Kacie Lamb

To Alfred Tennyson, My Grandson

Golden-hair'd Ally whose name is one with mine,
Crazy with laughter and babble and earth's
    new wine,
Now that the flower of a year and a half is thine,
O little blossom, O mine, and mine of mine,
Glorious poet who never hast written a line,
Laugh, for the name at the head of my verse
    is thine.
May'st thou never be wrong'd by the name that
    is mine!

— Alfred Tennyson

Why God
Made Little Boys

God made a world out of his dreams,
Of magic mountains, oceans and streams,
Prairies and plains and wooded land.
Then he paused and thought,
"I need someone to stand
On top of the mountains, to conquer the seas,
Explore the plains and climb the trees.
Someone to start out small and grow,
Sturdy, strong like a tree," and so…

He created boys full of spirit and fun,
To explore and conquer, to romp and run,
With dirty faces, banged up chins,
With courageous hearts and boyish grins.
When He had completed the task He'd begun,
He surely said, "That's a job well done."

— Author Unknown

Advice for Your Life Journey

There are many decisions that you will have to make in life. Choose wisely.

There are many opportunities that will present themselves in fancy wrapping, but they may not be the best for you.

There are a few opportunities that come wrapped in hard work, courage, and commitment. These will change your life.

Find your passions — those things that make you want to get out of bed in the morning with a spring in your step — and build your life around them.

Look inside your heart to find that which drives and propels you forward to make a difference in the lives of others. Add value wherever you go.

Choose your battles carefully. People will rub you the wrong way at times, but some problems are not worth the confrontation.

Faith is a key that will help you move mountains. Inner turmoil is a sure sign that you're on the wrong track. Know yourself, and let peace be your guide.

— Cindy Nicolson

Everywhere you journey in life, know that these are things I'll always hope and pray…

That the world will treat you fairly. That people will appreciate the one-in-a-million person you are. That you will be safe and smart and sure to make good choices on your journey through life. That a wealth of opportunities will come your way.

That your blessings will be many, your troubles will be few, and that life will be very generous in giving you all the happiness and success you deserve.

You're not just a fantastic grandson.
You're a tremendous, rare, and
extraordinary person. All the different
facets of your life — the ones you
reveal to the rest of the world and the
ones known only to those you're close
to — are so impressive. And as people
look even deeper, I know they can't help
but see how wonderful you are inside.

— Douglas Pagels

Remember...
Attitude Is Everything

Whatever you put out into the world is what comes back to you. If you only put negativity into the universe, you are unlikely to receive joyous things. But if you are positive and do good things, you will get good things in return.

Surround yourself with happy, productive, and generous people, and you will be inspired to be the same.

Study the people around you, and you will see how attitude reflects how their life is going. You will see a vast difference in the people who are happy and the ones who are not.

When you are grateful for everything that comes your way, you will find that you have more to be grateful for.

Attitude is everything in life.

— April Aragam

How Can You Measure the Value of a Man?

The measure of a man is not found in
the things he owns
or what he's saved for retirement
or even his accomplishments.

The true measure of a man is found in
his faith and in his heart.
It's found in the friends who stand by him,
the strength he displays under pressure,
the sensitivity he unashamedly expresses,
and his willingness to reveal vulnerability,
even at the risk of being hurt.

And it's found in the truth of his words,
    the genuineness of his life,
    his unselfish actions,
    and the values he lives by.

Determine the measure of a man
    not by admiring his trophies
    or by comparing him to other men
    who are either weaker or stronger.

Determine the measure of a man
    by how much you trust him
      and believe in him
    and by how much his life
      enhances yours.
                   — Craig Brannon

Grandfather's letter

by Steve Brunkhorst

One day, a young man was cleaning out his late grandfather's belongings when he came across a bright red envelope. Written on the front were the words, "To my grandson." Recognizing his grandfather's writing, the boy opened the envelope. A letter inside read…

Dear Grandson,

Years ago you came to me for help. You said, "Grandpa, how is it that you've accomplished so much in your life? You're still full of energy, and I'm already tired of struggling. How can I get that same enthusiasm that you've got?"

I didn't know what to say to you then. But knowing my days are numbered, I figure that I owe you an answer. So here is what I believe.

I think a lot of it has to do with how a person looks at things. I call it "keeping your eyes wide open."...

First, realize that life is filled with surprises, but many are good ones. If you don't keep watching for them, you'll miss half the excitement. Expect to be thrilled once in a while, and you will be.

When you meet up with challenges, welcome them. They'll leave you wiser, stronger, and more capable than you were the day before. When you make a mistake, be grateful for the things it taught you. Resolve to use that lesson to help you reach your goals.

And always follow the rules — even the little ones. When you follow the rules, life works. If you think you ever really get by with breaking the rules, you're only fooling yourself.

It's also important to decide exactly what you want. Then keep your mind focused on it, and be prepared to receive it.

But be ready to end up in some new places too. As you grow with the years, you'll be given bigger shoes to fill. So be ready for endings as well as challenging beginnings.

Sometimes we have to be brave enough to move from the familiar to the unfamiliar. Life isn't just reaching peaks. Part of it is moving from one peak to the next. If you rest too long in between, you might be tempted to quit. Leave the past in the past. Climb the next mountain and enjoy the view.

Dump things that weigh you down emotionally and spiritually. When an old resentment, belief, or attitude becomes heavy, lighten your load. Shed those hurtful attitudes that slow you down and drain your energy.

Remember that your choices will create your successes and your failures. So consider all the pathways ahead, and decide which ones to follow. Then believe in yourself, get up, and get going.

And be sure to take breaks once in a while. They'll give you a renewed commitment to your dreams and a cheerful, healthy perception of the things that matter the most to you.

Most important of all, never give up on yourself. The person who ends up a winner is the one who resolves to win. Give life everything you've got, and life will give its best back to you.

Love always, Grandpa

Believe in Yourself and Your Dreams

Dreams can come true if you take the time to
think about what you want in life
Get to know yourself
Find out who you are
Choose your goals carefully
Be honest with yourself
Find many interests and pursue them
Find out what is important to you
Find out what you are good at
Don't be afraid to make mistakes
Work hard to achieve successes
When things are not going right
don't give up — just try harder
Find courage inside of you to remain strong
Give yourself freedom to try out new things
Don't be so set in your ways that you can't grow

Always act in an ethical way
Laugh and have a good time
Form relationships with people you respect
Treat others as you want them to treat you
Be honest with people
Accept the truth
Speak the truth
Open yourself up to love
Don't be afraid to love
Remain close to your family
Take part in the beauty of nature
Be appreciative of all that you have
Help those less fortunate than you
Try to make other lives happy
Work toward peace in the world
Live life to the fullest
Grandson, dreams can come true
and I hope that your dreams become a reality

— Susan Polis Schutz

Live Your Life Purpose

Stay curious. Give wings to your dreams. Make friends with who you are. Grow your own happiness one day at a time. Imagine your own tomorrow and visualize your special star shining brightly. There are a thousand open doors waiting out there for you. Take a chance and explore your potential. There is so much to see. You have so much to give. Life is full of wonderful, beautiful, amazing miracles… and you're one of them.

Celebrate living every day. Leave your own set of footprints wherever life leads. Things change sometimes, so stay prepared. Widen your horizons. Dream deeply, with passion and purpose. Do the things you want to do. Light your own candle. Let a strong, deep faith be your guide. Let whatever inspires you lead you on and all you wish for be yours.

There are so many great things about you. There is the way you believe in yourself and in others. There is the way you fulfill your potential and help others find theirs. No one is more deserving of happiness than you. Treat yourself to all the joy life has for you. Your heart holds so many treasures — go ahead and reach for all of them. Do the things that bring out the rainbow in you. Every dawn is a gift with your name written on it. May life surprise you with joy everywhere.

— Linda E. Knight

Don't Be in a Rush

Why should we be in such desperate haste to succeed and in such desperate enterprises? If a man does not keep pace with his companions, perhaps it is because he hears a different drummer. Let him step to the music he hears, however measured or far away.

— Henry David Thoreau

Remember that there is plenty of time
to travel another road —
    and still another —
in your journey through life.
Take the time to find the route
that is right for you.

— Jacqueline Schiff

When you encounter difficulties
    and contradictions,
do not try to break them,
but bend them with gentleness and time.

— St. Francis de Sales

Every Life Has Its Ups and Downs

Life will always have disappointments
and heartaches.
It never stays happy, and just as important,
it never stays sad.
Anger has its place, too,
yet it should be controlled and let go.
Happiness is almost always a state of mind
and an attitude that can be controlled
in most situations.

Choose happiness when at all possible.
Keep good memories and discard hurts
and failures.
Allow yourself to make mistakes
and realize that's when you may learn
your biggest lessons.

— Barbara Cage

Ten Things Every Man Should Keep in Mind at All Times

1. Right-y, tight-y; left-y, loose-y.

2. A career is not a substitute for a life plan.

3. Shouting doesn't help.

4. Laughter does.

5. It is inevitable that the people you love will occasionally let you down.

6. It is inevitable that you will occasionally let down the people you love.

7. Health is the first wealth.

8. It takes too much energy to hold a grudge.

9. Amortize, ameliorate, or purge all regrets every five years.

10. Flowers always help. So does "I'm sorry" and "Thanks."

— Jake Morrissey

The Secrets of Lasting Happiness

One of the secrets of happiness is to take time to accomplish what you have to do, then to make time to achieve what you want to do.

Remember that life is short. Its golden moments need hopes and memories and dreams. When it seems like those things are lost in the shuffle, you owe it to yourself to find them again. The days are too precious to let them slip away.

If you're working too hard, make sure it's because it's a sacrifice for a time when you're going to pay yourself back with something more important than money could ever be. If you're losing the battle, do what it takes to win the war over who is in control of your destiny.

Find time, make time, take time... to do something rewarding and deeply personal and completely worthwhile. Time is your fortune, and you can spend it to bring more joy to yourself and to others your whole life through.

— Collin McCarty

Take Time To...

Lean against a tree
and dream your world of dreams
Work hard at what you like to do
and try to overcome all obstacles
Laugh at your mistakes
and praise yourself for learning from them
Pick some flowers
and appreciate the beauty of nature
Be honest with people
and enjoy the good in them

Don't be afraid to show your emotions
Laughing and crying make you feel better
Love your friends and family with your
    entire being
They are the most important part of your life
Feel the calmness on a quiet sunny day
and plan what you want to accomplish in life
Find a rainbow
and live your
world of dreams

— Susan Polis Schutz

Build Good Character

Character is not something you were born with and can't change, like your fingerprint. In fact, because you weren't born with it, it is something that you must take responsibility for creating.... Character is built by how you respond to what happens in your life. Whether it's winning every game or losing every game. Getting rich or dealing with hard times. You build character out of certain qualities that you must create and diligently nurture within yourself. Just like you would plant and water a seed or gather wood and build a campfire. You've got to look for those things in your heart and in your gut. You've got to chisel away in order to find them. Just like chiseling away the rock in order to create the sculpture that has previously existed only in your imagination.

— Jim Rohn

No matter what you undertake in life,
do so with a joyful and positive attitude.
Work hard and try your best, pouring your
heart into all you do. Demonstrate sincere
gratitude and don't take your loved ones
for granted. Don't just "follow the crowd";
stand firm in maintaining your individuality.

— Debbie Burton-Peddle

Hold yourself responsible for a higher
standard than anybody else expects
of you. Never excuse yourself.

— Henry Ward Beecher

You've Got Choices

When you have something particularly challenging to deal with, try to remind yourself…

You've got this moment… You can choose to be happy or unhappy. You can choose what you think, what you say, and how you feel. You can choose to be hopeful or hopeless, to respond angrily or cheerfully, to be bored or interested.

You've got this day… No matter what the weather is like, you can choose what kind of day it will be — beautiful or awful or somewhere in between. You can choose what you will do and what you won't — to give up or give in or go on. You have a choice to do something or nothing, to start now or later. You can choose your attitude about what you're facing.

You've got your life… If you're not happy, satisfied, encouraged, and hopeful, you're cheating yourself. You can talk and talk to yourself about what you need to do to honor your life, but if you don't turn those thoughts into actions, you're just playing games and giving up to whatever comes to mind.

You've got the power to make choices… Your life is the manifestation of the choices you make each moment and each day. When you use this awesome gift to your best advantage, there is nothing you can't do.

— Donna Fargo

I Know You Will Be a Success

What does it mean to succeed? Most people see success as being rich and famous or powerful and influential. Others see it as being at the top of their profession and standing out from the rest.

The wise see success in a more personal way; they see it as achieving the goals they have set for themselves, and then feeling pride and satisfaction in their accomplishments. True success is felt in the heart, not measured by money and power.

So be true to yourself and achieve
the goals you set. For success is
reaching those goals and feeling proud
of what you have accomplished.

— Tim Tweedie

What Is a Man?

A man is someone who realizes
that strength of character is
more important than being tough.
A man can be tender and kind, and
he doesn't misuse his authority.
He is generous and enjoys
giving as well as receiving.
He is understanding: he tries to
see both sides of a situation.
He is responsible: he knows what
needs to be done, and he does it.
He is trustworthy: his word is his honor.

He loves humor and looks at
   the bright side of things.
He takes time to think
   before he reacts.
He loves life, nature, discovery,
   excitement, and so much more.
He is a little boy sometimes, living
   in an adult body, and enjoying
   the best of both worlds.

— Barbara Cage

If —

If you can keep your head when all about you
    Are losing theirs and blaming it on you;
If you can trust yourself when all men doubt you,
    But make allowance for their doubting too;
If you can wait and not be tired by waiting,
    Or being lied about, don't deal in lies,
Or being hated, don't give way to hating,
    And yet don't look too good, nor talk too wise;

If you can dream — and not make dreams your master;
    If you can think — and not make thoughts your aim,
If you can meet with Triumph and Disaster
    And treat those two impostors just the same;
If you can bear to hear the truth you've spoken
    Twisted by knaves to make a trap for fools,
Or watch the things you gave your life to, broken,
    And stoop and build 'em up with worn-out tools;

If you can make one heap of all your winnings
	And risk it on one turn of pitch-and-toss,
And lose, and start again at your beginnings
	And never breathe a word about your loss;
If you can force your heart and nerve and sinew
	To serve your turn long after they are gone,
And so hold on when there is nothing in you
	Except the Will which says to them: "Hold on!"

If you can talk with crowds and keep your virtue,
	Or walk with Kings — nor lose the common touch,
If neither foes nor loving friends can hurt you,
	If all men count with you, but none too much;
If you can fill the unforgiving minute
	With sixty seconds' worth of distance run,
Yours is the Earth and everything that's in it,
	And — which is more — you'll be a Man, my son!

— Rudyard Kipling

Always Have Hope

Don't let go of hope.
Hope gives you the strength to keep going
when you feel like giving up.
Don't ever quit believing in yourself.
As long as you believe you can,
you will have a reason for trying.
Don't let anyone hold your happiness
    in their hands;
hold it in yours, so it will always
    be within your reach.
Don't measure success or failure
    by material wealth,
but by how you feel;
our feelings determine the richness of
    our lives.
Don't let bad moments overcome you;
be patient, and they will pass.
Don't hesitate to reach out for help;
we all need it from time to time.

Don't run away from love,
    but toward love,
because it is our deepest joy.
Don't wait for what you want
    to come to you.
Go after it with all that you are,
knowing that life will meet you halfway.
Don't feel like you've lost
when plans and dreams fall short of
    your hopes.
Anytime you learn something new
about yourself or about life,
you have progressed.
Don't do anything that takes away
from your self-respect.
Feeling good about yourself
is essential to feeling good about life.
Don't ever forget how to laugh
or be too proud to cry.
It is by doing both that we live life
    to its fullest.
                    — Nancye Sims

When You Sail, Kiss the Waters

If you do great things, do them greatly
and keep them rooted in the ways of greatness
When you walk, walk aright
When you kneel, bow your head
For deep love from afar has carried you here
and it is the only way home

If you love someone, love them all
from the tops of their heads to the
    soles of their feet
and don't worry that they may not love you back
The giving of love makes the greatness of love
and it is the only way home

If you must fall, fall straight to your knees
You will learn how to stand on your feet
by the fear in your heart
the sweat on your face
and the love that beats strong in your chest

When you sail, kiss the waters
When you fly, talk to God
When you run, lay claim to spirits
When you walk, face the wind
When you reach, touch a cloud
    or a cobweb
Then touch them again

When you watch, take your time
When you turn, trust the way
and listen for angels to speak
You will see the unseen
in the place of unseens
if you listen for words in between

When you're happy, swim in it
When you're troubled, swim through it
When you're fearful, swim over it
When you love, drown in it
When you hurt, hold my hand
And don't ever forget
that love is the only way home

               — Mimi Lenox

You'll Always Have Me to Care About You

No one ever really knows
what life has in store,
what roads lie ahead,
or how things will turn out.

It's kind of scary sometimes,
looking ahead and not knowing,
but I want you to know
that you'll always have me.
It doesn't matter where I am
or what I'm doing;
I will always take time for you.

You have a place in my heart
that will always be there for you.

— Beth Fagan Quinn

There are probably far too many things in my life that I take for granted. But you will never, ever be one of them. I know how blessed I am to have you here. In every way. I am proud of you to the nth degree, and I can't help thinking of what utter and absolute joy I would have missed… if I hadn't had the gift… of you in my life.

You will always be my special guy. And I will always be so grateful for you.

— Terry Bairnson

If I Could, Grandson...

If I could bring you a world full of happiness, I would. If I could take your sadness and pain and feel them for you, I would. If I could give you the strength to handle the problems that this world may have for you, I'd do that too. There is nothing that I wouldn't do for you to bring laughter instead of tears into your life.

I can't give you happiness, but I can feel it with you. I can't take away all your hurts in this world, but I can share them with you. I can't give you strength when you need it the most, but I can try to be strong for you.

I can be there to tell you how much I love you. In times when you feel you need to reach out to someone, I can be there for you, not to change how you feel, but to go through these times with you.

When you were little, I could hold you in my arms to comfort you, but you'll never be too grown up for me to put my arms around you. You are so very special to me, and the most precious gift I could have ever received was you on the day you were born.

— Millie P. Lorenz

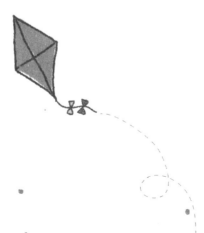

We'll Always Be Close

Our feelings of closeness
will never be limited
by the time we spend apart.
Homes and families
as precious as ours
can only be comprised of
    near and caring feelings.
Our family is such an essential
    part of our lives
that the caring will never leave us.
The love we share resides
    continually in our hearts.

— Andrew Tawney

You and I cannot be separated.
We're far too close for that.
We will always be together,
even when I'm not close enough
    to give you a hug,
and we will live in
    each other's heart forever.

— Nancy Hazel Davis

A Blessing
for Our Family

May our family be blessed with
   comforts of the physical
      and riches of the spirit.
May our paths be lit with sunshine
   and sorrow ne'er darken our doors.
May our harvest be bountiful
   and our hearth ever welcoming.
May we celebrate together in times of joy
   and comfort one another
      in times of sorrow.
And mostly:
May we always stay together
   and share the laughter, the love, and the tears
      as only family can.

— Danielle Brigante

A Blessing
for You, Grandson

As you travel this path of life,
may the sun warm
the ground beneath your feet.
May the wind move
the gray clouds behind you,
and may the stars' light
break up the darkness.
May angels guide your steps
and fill your soul with peace,
and may love greet you
at every crossroad.

— Tammy Bennett

Don't Ever Forget How Special You Are

Your presence is a present to the world ✳ You're unique and one of a kind ✳ Your life can be what you want it to be ✳ Take the days just one at a time ✳ Count your blessings, not your troubles ✳ You'll make it through whatever comes along ✳ Within you are so many answers ✳ Understand, have courage, be strong ✳ Don't put limits on yourself ✳ So many dreams are waiting to be realized ✳ Decisions are too important to leave to chance ✳ Reach for your peak, your goal, your prize ✳

Nothing wastes more energy than worrying *
The longer one carries a problem, the heavier
it gets * Don't take things too seriously *
Live a life of serenity, not a life of regrets *
Remember that a little love goes a long way *
Remember that a lot goes forever * Remember
that friendship is a wise investment * Life's
treasures are people... together * Realize
that it's never too late * Do ordinary things
in an extraordinary way * Have health and
hope and happiness * Take the time to wish
upon a star * And don't ever forget... for
even a day... how very special you are *

— Douglas Pagels

I Feel So Fortunate
to Have You for
a Grandson

I love your bright face
when we talk seriously about the world
I love your smile
when you laugh at the inconsistencies
  in the world
I love your eyes
when you are showing emotion
I love your mind
when you are discovering new ideas
and creating dreams to follow

I enjoy you so much and
I look forward to any time
we can spend together
Not only are you my adored grandson
but you are also my friend

— Susan Polis Schutz

Grandson, These Are the Gifts I Wish for You...

The gift of knowing that it's people like you who make life so sweet… for people like me.

All your friends and loved ones, from close by and miles away, gathered together to celebrate all the amazing things about you!

Happiness that simply overflows… from memories made, peacefulness within, and the anticipation of so many good things to come.

Days that shine so bright and wishing stars that come out at night and listen to everything your heart is hoping for.

Paths ahead that take you all the places
you want to be and that bring you closer
to all the great things you deserve.

The kind of joy that you always give to others…
coming back to bless you all through the year.

And reminders that in so many ways, you
are such a wonderful gift, and one of the
nicest things in this entire world…
is your presence in it.

— Jordan Carrill

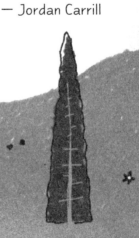

I wish you...

A reverent spirit full of wonder — with eyes, ears, and heart open to the miracles of beauty all around you. The most beautiful things in life are free: sunrises and sunsets, rainbows — especially double ones! — fields of wildflowers, ripples in a pond, the ocean's roar, the choruses of bird songs and children singing, a child's cooing and smile, the breeze, and the dances of trees. Love and protect nature. Listen to and really see it. I'm always amazed at how much I do not see in my busyness and preoccupation. So be still and just be as often as you can....

A compassionate spirit. Listen. See. Hear. Feel. Seek to understand. Care. Share with those in need. If you try to live a life of compassion and faith that seeks justice, God will smile on you....

A resilient spirit. Don't dwell on your failures. Learn from them and move on. It does not matter how many times you fall down, keep getting up. You are going to make mistakes but try not to keep making the same ones. Don't dwell on your weaknesses or on what you wish you could do but can't. Do what you can do. Build on your strengths. You have many that are unique to you. Don't compare yourself to your sister or brother or cousins or friends or parents or grandparents. Just try to be the best possible you. There is not a single other person like you in the whole world. Don't make excuses. Prepare and do what you've got to do. If you didn't prepare, say so, apologize, take the consequences, and do better next time....

A loving spirit that wells up in wonder and laughter and newness your whole life because you know you are loved. You already have it. Nurture it. Love is the most important value in life. Love of God, of self, and of your neighbor as yourself.

— Marian Wright Edelman

Grandson, I Love You with All My Heart

The things we share are so special to me;
I'll cherish them for a lifetime.
Spending time with you is something
I've always looked forward to
ever since you were a baby.

You've added so much joy to my life.
Though we come from different generations,
our hearts share the same laughter
and the same love.
Those are two things in life
that age cannot change.

If I could tell you a million times a day
that I love you — and hug you just as much —
that still would never be enough
to express just how much you mean to me.
I hope you are reminded of my love for you
in some small ways throughout your life.

My love is a legacy I leave to you.
I want you to know I wish
the very best for you always.
Being a part of your life is
a blessing and a privilege.

— Dianne Cogar

Acknowledgments

We gratefully acknowledge the permission granted by the following authors, publishers, and authors' representatives to reprint poems or excerpts from their publications.

Susan Hickman Sater for "There has never been...." Copyright © 2014 by Susan Hickman Sater. All rights reserved.

Dianne Cogar for "I've Loved You Since the Minute You Were Born." Copyright © 2014 by Dianne Cogar. All rights reserved.

Curtis Brown, Ltd., for "Grandchildren... rekindle for us the spirit..." from A BOOK FOR GRANDMOTHERS by Ruth Goode. Copyright © 1976 by Ruth Goode. All rights reserved.

Alan Beck for "What Is a Boy?" Copyright © 1950 by Alan Beck and New England Mutual Life Insurance Company. All rights reserved.

Gail Fishman Gerwin for "My Grandson Learns How to Punctuate" from DEAR KINFOLK, published by ChayaCairn Press. Copyright © 2012 by Gail Fishman Gerwin. All rights reserved.

Candy Paull for "Grandson, You Are Meant for Greatness." Copyright © 2012 by Candy Paull. All rights reserved.

Cindy Nicolson for "Advice for Your Life Journey." Copyright © 2014 by Cindy Nicolson. All rights reserved.

April Aragam for "Remember... Attitude Is Everything." Copyright © 2014 by April Aragam. All rights reserved.

Steve Brunkhorst for "Grandfather's Letter." Copyright © 2005 by Steve Brunkhorst. All rights reserved.

Linda E. Knight for "Live Your Life Purpose." Copyright © 2014 by Linda E. Knight. All rights reserved.

Scribner, a division of Simon and Schuster, Inc., for "Ten Things Every Man Should Keep in Mind at All Times" by Jake Morrissey from A MAN'S JOURNEY TO SIMPLE ABUNDANCE by Sarah Ban Breathnach and Friends, edited by Michael Segell. Copyright © 2000 by Simple Abundance, Inc. All rights reserved.

Jim Rohn for "Character is not something..." from Jim Rohn Weekly E-zine, Issue 97, August 21, 2001, www.JimRohn.com. Copyright © 2001 by Jim Rohn. All rights reserved.

PrimaDonna Entertainment Corp. for "You've Got Choices" by Donna Fargo. Copyright © 2010 by PrimaDonna Entertainment Corp. All rights reserved.

Mimi Lenox for "When You Sail, Kiss the Waters" from Mimi Writes... (blog), March 22, 2012, www.mimiwrites.blogspot.com. Copyright © 2012 by Mimi Lenox. All rights reserved.

Danielle Brigante for "A Blessing for Our Family" from FAMILY CELEBRATIONS: PRAYERS, POEMS, AND TOASTS FOR EVERY OCCASION by June Cotner. Copyright © 1999 by Danielle Brigante. All rights reserved.

Hachette Book Group for "I wish you..." from THE SEA IS SO WIDE AND MY BOAT IS SO SMALL by Marian Wright Edelman. Copyright © 2008 by Marian Wright Edelman. Reprinted by permission. All rights reserved.

A careful effort has been made to trace the ownership of selections used in this anthology in order to obtain permission to reprint copyrighted material and give proper credit to the copyright owners. If any error or omission has occurred, it is completely inadvertent, and we would like to make corrections in future editions provided that written notification is made to the publisher:

BLUE MOUNTAIN ARTS, INC., P.O. Box 4549, Boulder, Colorado 80306.